Changing Paris

Changing Paris

A TOUR ALONG THE SEINE

PHOTOGRAPHS BY

PHILIP TRAGER

ARCHITECTURAL COMMENTARY

Thomas Mellins

FOREWORD

Pierre Borhan

INTRODUCTION

Diane Johnson

ARENA EDITIONS

First Edition published by Arena Editions

573 West San Francisco Street

Santa Fe, New Mexico 87501 USA

505.986.9132 TELEPHONE   505.986.9138 FACSIMILE

www.arenaeditions.com

Library of Congress Catalog Card Number: 99-073752

Hardcover ISBN: 1-892041-21-9

Limited Edition ISBN: 1-892041-23-5

Distributed by D.A.P./Distributed Art Publishers

155 Sixth Avenue

New York, NY 10013

212.627.1999

PRINTED IN ITALY

FIRST EDITION

1 2 3 4 5 6 7 8 9

for Ina

Kindred spirit, enthusiastic companion, translator,
seeker of permits and pursuer of sites, skies and sunsets

CONTENTS

LIST OF PHOTOGRAPHS BY PLATE NUMBER

FOREWORD

PIERRE BORHAN

Philip Trager is one of the few photographers of his generation to dedicate himself almost exclusively to architectural photography: The genre has not really found a place in mainstream photography, making it difficult sometimes for its practitioners to make a living from their artwork alone. It requires great sacrifice, but only grudgingly allots its rewards of financial success and recognition.

Free of the expectation of public acknowledgment, Philip Trager photographed Wesleyan University, which he attended; the skyscrapers of New York; and, in Italy, Palladio's villas. Although he would certainly have earned more had he given other form to his thoughts, desires, and fantasies, he persevered, spending long periods in 1994 and 1995 in the architecturally handsome areas of Paris.

Trager is well versed in the history of photography, and more specifically in the development of photographic representation of the French capital from Daguerre's time on, yet he blazed a path independently of both his early forebears—including the masters he admires—and his fellow photographers. Nor did he favor the ancient winding alleys over the new commercial centers, opting instead to track the eastward progression of the great buildings over the last decades.

This was a natural choice for a foreigner intrigued by the works of Dominique Perrault (Bibliothèque Nationale de France François Mitterrand) and I.M. Pei (Pyramide du Louvre). Of course, as he pursued his trail, he also captured Notre-Dame de Paris, Pont Alexandre III, and the Palais de Chaillot, but it was the *Grands Projets* that captivated his photographer's eye, from the quarter of La Défense, with its monumental arch, to the Ministère des Finances, designed by Paul Chemetov and built in Bercy in the 1980s. The new geometrical edifices—which tend to be simple, pure, and at times a little heavy, despite the increased use of glass—became for him, as for other visitors and indeed the Parisians themselves, new landmarks and new symbols. Where Eugène Atget may appear addicted to the past, Trager—though not obsessed by progress per se, by all those works that are (or try to be) extraordinary or eccentric—cared to record many of the new architectural works, whether he admired them or not. He was perfectly aware that the Louvre Pyramid, conceived as a luminous counterpart to the opaque and mysterious Egyptian pyramids, punctuates the history of architecture, which is, like all history, made of renewals and mutations.

Trager's architectural Paris is part of the tourists' Paris, with its historical monuments, museums, great buildings, and public gardens . . . but without the tourists: he has scrupulously avoided any human presence. Each photograph gives priority to the building he chose, to its conception and ground plan, rather than to its social purpose or use. What commands his attention is the power of a site, a façade, an esplanade, or the punctuation that a sculpture can supply. This unpicturesque Paris, devoid of daily life, gives unambiguous proof of Trager's emotional neutrality. He could have mourned the destruction of Les Halles conceived by Victor Baltard or of the Bercy warehouses, and cursed the evils of the industrial ages and other pollutions—street signs and advertisements—but such judgments, such states of mind, are not natural to him. Photographically, he also forbade himself all grandiloquent lyricism, both complaint and enthusiasm. Between the lost, disfigured, and ravaged Paris grieved by the Ancients, and the more structured, functional, airy Paris vaunted by the Moderns, Trager retains the freedom of a spectator, a citizen of the world.

Rather than wander through Paris at the whim of his personal taste, Trager used the Seine as his guideline, the axis of his carefully considered itinerary, which he methodically defined and followed. For him, however, the quays and bridges, the Jardin des Tuileries, the Place du Vert-Galant, and the Île Saint-Louis are not dreamy places, as they were for André Kertész, Izis, Edouard Boubat, and the many others who were stirred by lovers, a fisherman, a hobo, a dead tree, a shadow, a reflection. Trager's is not the compassionate gaze known as "humanist." There is no melancholy in him as he raises his eyes to the buildings, major landmarks in the city's topography, rather than focusing on the passersby, the props, everything that usually makes up the urban landscape. His Paris, stripped of local color, contains no reference whatever to the customs of the times. His gaze is mastered, clarified, recalling photography's earliest days.

Trager is a direct descendant of the masters of the calotype, who exercised their talents between 1845 and 1860: Edouard Baldus, Henri Le Secq, and Gustave Le Gray, for whom architecture was a model. He is well within their lineage, that of the Heliographic Mission of 1851, and that of Pierre-Ambrose Richebourg, Louis De Clercq, the Bisson frères, even that of the Italian Domenico Bresolin and the German Jakob August Lorent. Trager prefers "objective realism" to any Pictorialism, Surrealism, Futurism, or Poetism. He does not revel in Baroque art. His photographic references are European rather than American, and historical— mid-nineteenth century—rather than contemporary. He loves sobriety (of form, materials, and spaces), order, and harmony, and eliminates all autobiographical clues from his photography. He has made his own such canonical photographic values as the ability to bear witness and the creation of a memory.

Another aspect of Trager's approach is that he never goes to the construction sites. He never photographs buildings in progress, unlike Charles Marville and Louis-Emile Durandelle, who, in the nineteenth century, were commissioned to do so by the companies themselves. Trager arrives on the scene after the builders have finished their part, once the buildings are completed. He concentrates on the façades and sometimes on perspectives. His attitude is not that of a stroller idly following impressions and affections, but that of someone sure of a visual goal. On site, he keeps his distance, backing away from monumentality. He avoids anecdote and narratives, emphasizing shapes with his color chart of grays. As an independent photographer who alone selected his subject, deciding to develop it over a series of views, Trager himself determines the limits of his freedom of interpretation. Solely responsible for his choices, he is not an architectural photographer by profession, that is not his trade; he does it because he wants to, when he wants to, as he wants to, and he practices architectural photography because architecture suits his creative endeavor. More precisely: it suits him in itself, not because it lends itself to plays of light (Alvin Langdon Coburn and Alfred Stieglitz early in the century, then, later, Marcel Bovis, René-Jacques, Brassaï for nighttime atmosphere, and Gilbert Fastenaekens and Daniel Boudinet in the 1970s and 1980s) or to experimental, unbalanced, surprising shots (László Moholy-Nagy, Alexander Rodchenko, Germaine Krull, François Kollar). It suits him because of its purity, rigor, even austerity. And so he elects a neutral light that tends toward gray, rather than the high contrast—the expressionism—of blacks and whites.

The documentary dimension of these photographs exists above and beyond their artistic value. They convey memories, they describe, but they were not done merely to provide the topographic, architectural inventory of Paris in the 1990s. They are plastic propositions. The spirit of the different places emanates from them, unbound to the contingencies, the hazards of the present. To leave room for it, Trager erases as much as possible any excessive personal expression that might compromise the photographic transparency. He is a radical in that he withdraws, letting himself be enthralled by the model, its presence, and its aura—when there is one. This humility allows him to approach one of photography's extreme qualities: the quality located, in Jean-Claude Lemagny's phrase, "at the end of its obedience to reality." This same quality also permits Philip Trager to experience time in the least human of its dimensions: the experience of timelessness.

ARTIST'S PREFACE

PHILIP TRAGER

Changing Paris has been the most exciting and satisfying, as well as the most complex and difficult, project I have undertaken during my thirty-five years of making photographs.

For nearly seven years, my energies have been devoted to making these photographs and this book. The actual taking of the photographs, although relatively recent, seems now to have been many years ago. This disjointed sense of time is, I believe, caused by my need to be involved in all aspects of a project: spending weeks in the darkroom, feeling that only I can make silver gelatin prints that coax the best out of my negatives; making decisions about the sequencing, designing and printing of the book; obtaining and checking information about architects and sites; understanding new ways of bookmaking using electronic technology.

At times, I doubted if this project would ever be completed and wondered if I could successfully photograph a city that has been photographed so beautifully in the past. I worked as if I were thirty years younger, often fatigued to the point of twice having thought I had taken a photograph only to find that although I had chosen the view and pressed the cable release, the camera had not been pointed in the chosen direction.

Yet, the positive aspects of photographing in Paris have been paramount and lasting. When you work with a view camera in the streets day after day, you begin to understand a city in a new way; you absorb its architecture. You have unforgettable and transcending experiences: feeling that the sun will never set on the Seine after working from sunrise on a summer day; believing that the river and the luminous sky are a single source of light; watching the rapidly changing skies transform the buildings. In beginning to sequence the photographs coherently, I became increasingly aware of the interaction of great buildings and their surroundings. I began to understand that the photographs, taken solely for aesthetic reasons, might eventually serve as a historic record of the city. I realized that I had to deal with a complex urban environment, with its vehicles, people, wires, and signs. While photographing, I felt more times than I would have hoped for, a mixture of concentration and excitement, harmony and effortlessness. My vision expanded to embrace contemporary architecture and I realized that the project was evolving into a different book than I had envisioned. I began to comprehend the city in terms of a flow of architecture, rather than as solitary buildings; to understand that gray, "dull" light can often be the best light; to deepen my appreciation of parks and gardens, the sophisticated and inventive mix of plants and structures at the Bois de Boulogne and the newly completed Parc de Bercy and Parc André-Citroën; to confirm once again that I virtually always find only one or two "correct" views of any building or site. I learned to be patient while Ina seemingly endlessly pursued permits; to collaborate intuitively with her, rapidly setting up the view camera to capture fluid situations, at times overcoming difficulties of working in the rain or by the flooding river.

Almost without exception, Parisians responded to my undertaking with kindness, partially, perhaps, because they appreciated an American's sustained interest in the architecture of their city. Strangers helped with my forty pounds of equipment; security guards took me to see uniquely beautiful grand private interior rooms in public institutions; bartenders, after some explanation, agreed to lock up my camera cases with their beer and wine when I was too exhausted to carry them back to the hotel; undercover police quickly understood my good intentions.

When I started this project in 1993, a Parisian advised me that in France practical arrangements are difficult at first and become easier as matters proceed, but that in the United States everything appears to be easy in the beginning, but thereafter becomes more difficult. I found this to be true and cherish the relationships that evolved as the project proceeded.

Many other kind and generous people made this book possible. I am especially grateful to the architects who graciously permitted photographs of the buildings they designed to appear in the book. I am indebted to Pierre Borhan, Diane Johnson, and Thomas Mellins, whose excellent contributions have significantly enhanced *Changing Paris*. A special debt of gratitude is owed to Hélène Prevost for her intelligence and expertise in searching out information and obtaining permissions from architects and sculptors whose works I photographed. She correctly described her role as that of a "Sherlock Holmes."

Richard Goodman first brought to me the idea of photographing Paris; Constance Sullivan provided insightful advice and support, and Brian Hotchkiss and Peter Blaiwas gave me constant support and good counsel; all of them helped in the evolution of this book in countless ways.

I am most grateful to James Crump, my publisher, who believed in this book and made it possible, and to Elsa Kendall, Laura Addison, and Larissa Leclair, of Arena Editions. I thank Katy Homans for her sensitivity and keen design skills, and Robert Hennessey for the subtle and sensitive scans he made for the printer. I am grateful to David Fahey and Sal Lopes for their help, Dorothy Smith for her years of invaluable assistance, Henry Horenstein for his advice, and Roberta Leighton and Jeannette Hopkins for their insights and skills.

Thanks are due also to Bénédicte Chesnelong, Jane Ginsburg, and Patricia Chaban for help generously given, and to Jöelle Delaplace and Eugenio Maseda, Monica Antoine, Alain and Virginie Nouyrigat, Agnes Gautreau, and Guillaume and Deepa Rebière.

I am very grateful to my children, Michael, Mariella, Julie, and Christophe, for their constant encouragement and love. I am indeed fortunate to have a Parisian son-in-law, who introduced me to his friend Valérie Sueur, who graciously helped me in France.

I offer my warm gratitude to those who helped me in Paris: Michèle Audon and Jean-Pierre Pellissier, Théâtre des Champs-Élysées; Rosie Adone-Bordet, Mairie de Paris, Direction des Parcs, Jardins et Espaces verts de la Ville de Paris; Catherine Belanger, Chargée des Relations Extérieures au Musée du Louvre; Mme Chal, Directeur Général de l'Information et de la Communication à la Mairie de Paris; Michel Couderc, le Sécretaire Général de la Questure, Assemblée Nationale; Sophie Cot, Canal Plus; Farid Djouhri, President, Concorde International; Mme Fleurquin and Yves Pacon, Maison de Radio-France; Général Forray and Lieutenant Colonel Didier Joly, Palais de la Légion d'Honneur; Corinna Fuhrer, Dominique Perrault Architecte; Mme Galan, Chargée du VIP; Mary E. Gawronski, Cultural Attaché, United States Embassy; M. Grandchamp, Hippodrome de Longchamp; Charlotte La Cour Veyranne, Attachée de Communication à la Ville de Paris; Elisabeth Laurent, Chargée de la Communication au Musée du Louvre; Mme Adam Mouton, Architecte de l'Assemblée Nationale; Cecelia James Nicoleu, Special Project Coordinator, Cultural Affairs, French Embassy; M. Peultre; Martine Rigaud, Centre d'Information, Bibliothèque Nationale de France François Mitterrand; Michelle Thiery, Service de la Communication et des Relations avec la Presse, Assemblée Nationale; Patrick Weiser, Administrateur Adjoint, Jardin des Tuileries et Domaine National du Palais Royal; and my thanks to all the gracious people, whose names I do not know, who kindly helped me in so many ways while I was photographing in the streets of Paris.

INTRODUCTION

DIANE JOHNSON

In her little book *French Ways and Their Meaning*, Edith Wharton, arguing for American intervention in the First World War, holds that what we notice and respond to in Paris begins with "the universal existence of [French] taste, and of the standards it creates—it insists on. . . . [T]he French have always felt and reverenced the beauty of their rivers, and known the value, artistic and hygienic, of a beautiful and well-kept river-front in the heart of a crowded city. . . ."[1] Her view that this in itself is evidence of their superiority was meant to impress Americans with the value of France as an exemplary culture worth saving from the Germans, and maybe to inspire us to take care of our own rivers. Wharton particularly admired a stretch of the Seine which, as it happens, is near my Paris apartment:

> *[I]t would be difficult for anyone walking on the Quai Malaquais, and not totally blind to architectural beauty, not to be charmed by the harmony of proportion and beauty of composition of a certain building with curved wings and a small central dome that looks across the Seine at the gardens of the Louvre and the spires of Saint Germain l'Auxerrois. . . . That building, all elegance, measure and balance, from its graceful cupola to the stately stone vases surmounting the lateral colonnades. . . .*[2]

This is the Institut de France, begun in 1663. A few steps away, my building was probably constructed before 1650. If you lean out of the window (if you can ignore the diesel-fumed buses below) you see a view not so different from what the people who lived here in the seventeenth century would have seen; walking to the corner, the viewer can see an ensemble of structures more or less unchanged since then—the Pont-Neuf, begun in 1578; the Institut de France; the Louvre, itself begun in the Middle Ages. From here Wharton would also have seen, but did not choose to mention, La Samaritaine department store on the right bank facing the Pont-Neuf (plate 44). It is not the store standing today, which was built in 1927, but an earlier one, built in 1905. To Wharton, writing during the First World War, the 1927 building might have appeared garishly modern; to us, it looks like a dignified nineteenth-century one, diffidently harmonizing with its seventeenth-century neighbors, and even with the sixteenth-century Pont-Neuf, whose newly cleaned gargoyles scowl now as menacingly as then. Of course there are everywhere tiny vestiges of today—a modernized window, a skylight, the tottering glass boxes that are the added top floors and roof decks housing a community of residents living above Paris the way certain tribes live in the canopies of forests. Though the modern mixes with the ancient elsewhere along this river, right here is little evidence of the modern except for motor vehicles just visible on the opposite quay, tiny and ephemeral beside the pale stone monuments. One wonders how, and why, this stretch of river has avoided more serious change, and how it has reconciled the disparate aesthetics of several centuries.

The river itself reflects life in all its modern utility. The waters of the Seine are high in the winter seasons, when there have been heavy rains, and cover the cobbled walkways along the quays, covering even the stone benches put there for people to sit and contemplate the always fascinating animation of the river. The water, heavy with silt, is the same pale brown color as the stone parapets that line its banks. (Sometimes it is black or silver, but I have never seen it blue.) To control the occasional floods, to facilitate its historic function as a port, and for beauty's sake, the quays are lined with stone walls, imposing and high, quite unlike the banks of American rivers consecrated to commerce and manufactories. France, of course, was until fairly recently the province of kings who could ignore the imperatives that drive brasher upstart societies.

In Paris, contemplation is an encouraged public activity, and a *lieu de contemplation* formed part of the 1998 brief for architects and engineers competing for the job of building yet another footbridge across the river upstream behind the Pont de Bercy (34), to link the recently opened Bibliothèque Nationale de France François Mitterrand (34, 35) with the Promenade Arthur Rimbaud on the right bank. (Besides the bridge at Bercy, the city is also just completing a new footbridge between the Musée d'Orsay and the Jardin des Tuileries.) Someone walking across one of the many bridges over the Seine sees the houseboats, which never seem to move, lining the quay up and down the length of the city.

The Bateaux Mouches (Trager has caught one in plate 48)—flat tourist boats with two decks of seats, sometimes with dining rooms and dance floors—are almost the only boats one can see being boats as they hurry on their circuit past Notre-Dame, the two Îles (Cité and Saint-Louis), and the Pont-Neuf. Loudspeakers announce these monuments, and, at night, the lights from the boat illuminate the great Cathedral, the Conciergerie, the Louvre, with daylight brightness so that people whose apartments look onto the river must close their shutters at night if they wish to avoid the blinding intrusion of the lights into their bedrooms.

In speaking of the *paysage du fleuve*, the landscape of the river, as it was put in the brief for the footbridge competition, the Ville de Paris expresses its idea that it is the duty of the builders along it to facilitate *promenades*, *contemplation de la Seine*, and all this activity. Architects planning to build a new bridge across an American river would be told to facilitate automobile traffic, often excluding footways and bicycle paths.

People walk over—but no one swims in, rows, canoes, speeds or sails on—the Seine, though no one says why. Sometimes people answer that it is the pollution, or that it is unsafe; some say the noise is prohibited by ordinance. Signs on the bridges tell what to do if someone falls or jumps into the water, but I have never heard of this happening, though it is true that the daily newspapers do not dispirit their readers with the news of everyday tragedy or local murder—unless especially lurid and public in its implication. Though fishing has been announced to be safe, one suspects it may not be the custom to bathe in the river, and Parisians are bound by custom, which is part of the reason their city has survived more or less intact, and explains the delicacy with which they augment, garnish, enlarge, while preserving the harmony of their surroundings.

For the French have an attitude toward the *patrimoine*, the idea that bridges and buildings, and even the look of things are the collective property of French citizens—an indefinable share they all have in the beauty and appearance of the city, more or less the attitude that Edith Wharton would encourage in Americans. Public outcry is said to have stopped Georges Pompidou in his plan to raze part of the stretch along the river on the left bank for a motorway, a feat he accomplished on the right bank, answering objections by saying blithely, "Les français aiment la bagnole" ("The French love cars"). Public outcry also objected to the Tour Montparnasse once it was built (just visible in plate 12 behind the sculpture on the Hôtel de Coislin), and people could see the effect of skyscrapers in central Paris (so they were banned to the suburbs, where they sprout uncontrolled).

By what rules or instinct, then, is change introduced along this vital but timeless river? As we move upstream and downstream, we can see that there has been abundant change, modern and yet insistently French. For instance, the Louvre, most famously, has not at all avoided change, but has instead been the focus of it. Though most people seem to like, or at least accept the Pyramide, some do not. Far from exemplifying the "universal existence of taste," as Wharton liked to believe the French to possess, the Pyramide du Louvre (1–3) focused controversy and settled in the affirmative the daring proposition that monuments can be changed and tampered with.

Philip Trager's photographs of the Pyramide du Louvre dramatically show the power of the camera to ameliorate or glorify reality, and, equally, to notice something not quite working architecturally, which the photographer is apt silently to adjust. While one photograph (1) gives an objective account of the relative sizes of the large pyramidal structure flanked by small pyramids, in another (2) the camera angle augments the small auxiliary pyramid—in reality about one third the size of the big one—to seem nearly the same size as the big one, making them appear to be almost twin structures contrasted only in the different texture of their glass panes, with the original Louvre reflected therein. When a photographer's eye corrects the architect's, it comments, if only on itself.

Another example of the editorial eye of the photographer is seen in Trager's photo of Frank Gehry's American Center (63). Trager's eye is so sympathetic to architecture, so much the eye of a romantic about buildings, that for him, even the slightly disappointing Center, with its dumpy cladding of Parisian stone, becomes a photograph of a magic building bathed in light. What was an attempt by Gehry to allude to the traditional charm of Parisian buildings—based on his belief that their beauty comes from the uniformity of their stone, slate roofs and so forth—comes in Trager's interpretation to pertain more emphatically to the new Parisian building characterized by radiance.

A photograph is in fact never dispassionate; it can be satirical, romanticizing, or expressive, and Trager's photographs of Paris are supremely expressive of the spirit the French mean to give their public buildings, of *gloire* and permanence and humanity. The essential role of statuary to this endeavor is one of his most important perceptions. He has above all seen how the architecture of the Seine is inextricably bound up with sculpture, of lions and horses, urns, heraldic motifs, obelisks, and most usually of the human form. These shapely presences—pigeon-dropped and mossy, leaning over bridges, guarding entrances and palaces, lifting celebratory urns and globes—cavort the length of the river in Paris like river gods and goddesses, tutelary and beneficent. Sculpture is spiritually much more integral to a site than mere decoration; it is allegorical or celebrates history. Perhaps it is revealing that we say "mere" decoration, a reflex of our Puritan suspicion of ornament, while for the French, the three-dimensional object of decor is the material manifestation of the inner essence of things, and to lack it would be to be spiritually dead. The statues that have caught Trager's eye bring a human (or superhuman) energy to the austere stone of the banks; but more than this, these photographs document the metamorphosis in modern French buildings of the architecture itself, from decorated rectangular buildings into sculptural forms of their own, as in the curved planes of the Opéra Bastille. The buildings themselves are shaped as pyramid, arch, sphere, while representational sculpture disappears or becomes abstract. This can be clearly seen in the photograph of the Grande Arche de la Défense, with its welter of solid forms in the foreground.

One of the most fascinating illustrations of the integration of sculpture into the emotional life of France is the Flamme de la Liberté (26), whose subsequent odd fate is not revealed by the photograph. A gift to Paris conceived of by the *International Herald Tribune*, the flame is a replica of the flame carried by the Statue of Liberty in New York Harbor, itself a gift from France. Situated near the entrance to the tunnel where Princess Diana was killed, this gilded statue became in the minds of mourners a tribute to her, and is even thought to be the very "Candle in the Wind" mentioned in Elton John's memorial song. From the chaste form in the photograph it has evolved into the repository of sentimental effusions by visitors of all nationalities, as evidenced by the bouquets and notes pinned to it, and vigils at any hour.

We see statues in these photographs, but real humans are sternly excluded. How long Philip Trager must have waited to find a moment when there was almost no one in the Louvre, the most visited monument in

Paris. We don't see cars in these beautiful pictures; how that lightens the soul! In most of these photographs none can be seen in part, no doubt, owing to the patience of the photographer; but also because cars have actually been excluded from a number of these bridges, *passerelles*, *parvises* and so on—another testimony to the human orientation of the planners.

The Louvre, the Assemblée, the classic buildings along the Seine in the sixth and seventh *arrondissements* were built of Parisian stone, a lovely pale stone quarried not far from the city. A structure in stone is an enduring and solid affair, but stone limited the possibilities for building design until recently, when new materials changed the effect of the buildings ventured by modern architects working upstream and downstream from the center of historic Paris. The Parisians are proud, with good reason, of their *pierre de Paris*, often specifying its use as a condition of building, but one can't help but feel that one of the reasons for the Frank Gehry building being less admired than his subsequent Bilbao museum, is that he sacrificed daring to what he perceived as a traditional context.

In less sensitive locations, the modern architect usually has other materials at his disposal. The trend of the changing architecture is at the moment transparency. A decade ago it was mirrors, and buildings of mirrored glass belonging to television and radio stations surrounding the Parc André-Citroën (51–52), whose beautiful transparent rectangles exemplify the mood of present day builders. Mirrors worked toward the idea of invisibility, the idea of repeating the Seine and its surroundings rather than intruding. Besides reflecting the trees and sky, the mirror kept out heat, or kept it in; but now mirrored buildings strike the viewer as irritating and evasive, like someone keeping his sunglasses on while he talks to you.

The mirror is also a metaphor of cultural certitude not out of place in a society that doesn't mind looking at itself. By the same token, if building materials are metaphors, the transparency that the most recent buildings strive for, though congruent with what the French pride themselves on—clarity—does not consort with what we believe them to be—opaque and full of Byzantine complications.

One product of transparency is light. *Lumière*, as you would expect, is as much a part of the tradition of the City of Light as it is a quality of the new buildings. Trager has captured the extent to which light has played a part in the calculated effect of these structures insinuated among existing buildings. The dignified symmetry of classical façades has been augmented by radiance from glass, from light emanating from within buildings or through them, by the reflected sun or moon, and by reflections in the mirrored buildings surrounding them, all of this brilliantly photographed. Whatever its defects as a functioning library, the new Bibliothèque Nationale de France François Mitterrand (35) is glorious when it catches the rays of the afternoon sun. The Opéra Bastille, derided as a whale, is nearly a phantasm in Trager's photograph (5). These and other, less solid-looking, structures slip in like ghosts between existing monuments, with less disruption of the ensemble than that created by a work in stone—one need only think of the Met Life building in New York by way of horrible contrast. This incorporeal quality is something the architect counts on and the photographer celebrates, a property of daytime Paris.

But night falls. Medieval Paris was plunged into blackness as soon as the sun set. The night river in central Paris is still mostly dark, a black ribbon threading between dark banks, occasionally catching the moonlight. Street lamps over certain bridges make tiny festoons of light. But in the new *quartiers* in the fifteenth or sixteenth *arrondissements*, lights blaze out from within the glass buildings, from structures like the Maison de Radio-France, or we see the Opéra in its nighttime robe of light (5). And one imagines, inside the magnificent Parisian buildings, the splendor of myriad sumptuous rooms by candlelight, as in Philip Trager's interior photograph of the Palais de la Légion d'Honneur (21).

Notes

1. Edith Wharton, *French Ways and Their Meaning* (New York, D. Appleton & Co., 1919), 3.

2. Ibid., 43.

Changing Paris

The sequence of these photographs has been determined solely by aesthetic considerations.
A map locating each site follows the photographs.

When Marcel Duchamp emigrated from Paris to the United States in 1942, he took with him a glass jar full of the air of his beloved city. A Dadaist gesture par excellence, Duchamp's action was more than brilliantly absurdist; the artist's imported atmosphere speaks eloquently about Paris, a city whose soul is defined not just by its buildings, its people, and its history, but by the magically light-infused air that imbues a very real urban place with a dreamlike dimension.

Dreams express the limitlessness of the human imagination and the necessity of creativity; how fitting, then, that Paris, an inhabitable dreamscape, does not merely change, but perpetually charts new artistic ground. Those who build and shape Paris are not content to treat the city, no matter how steeped in history, as though it were a period room in a museum, every object permanently fixed in time and space; instead they add their dreams to a cityscape that continues to unfold, sometimes in ways that are firmly rooted in the city's illustrious architectural traditions, sometimes in ways that are startlingly new.

Though many of Paris's individual buildings are brilliant in concept and execution, they are perhaps not what most characterizes the city's built environment. Rather, it is arguably the relationship of those buildings to their physical and their cultural context that distinguishes Paris. In no other city do the constituent buildings so convincingly compose a cohesive physical whole and at the same time insistently reflect a belief in the ability of architecture to communicate a society's ideals.

Thus Paris is the city as site specific and the city as transcendent thought.

I
COUR NAPOLÉON,
MUSÉE DU LOUVRE
(1852)
Hector Martin Lefuel,
architect,
following plans by
Louis Tullius Visconti

PYRAMIDE
DU LOUVRE
(1989)
I.M. Pei, architect

2

PYRAMIDE DU LOUVRE (1989)

I.M. Pei, architect

If the traditional architecture of Paris constitutes a fantasy rendered in stone, the city's modern architecture to a large extent embodies a crystalline dream. I.M. Pei's glass pyramids—the most visible and remarkable part of his extensive alteration of the Louvre Museum—rise from the granite-paved Cour Napoléon. Framed by the museum's nineteenth-century Second Empire–style wings by Louis Tullius Visconti, the main pyramid rises seventy-one feet—roughly the height of the first cornice of Visconti's façades—and is surrounded by three smaller pyramidal structures, as well as fountains.

3
PYRAMIDE DU LOUVRE (1989)
I.M. Pei, architect

COUR NAPOLÉON, MUSÉE DU LOUVRE (1852)
Hector Martin Lefuel, architect, following plans by Louis Tullius Visconti

At once enclosing and slicing through the Paris air, Pei's glass monument is meticulously wrought.
In the principal structure, 118 triangular and 675 diamond panes are held in place by 128 steel girders
in turn supported by 16 steel cables placed in a "bowstring" arrangement that was masterminded by a
manufacturer of sailboat rigging used on America's Cup yachts. The structures' forms are dramatic,
but their transparency allows them to take a surprisingly uncompetitive stance toward the existing
building. Pei's masterwork is indeed a rare architectural entity: an accommodating icon.

4
OPÉRA BASTILLE (1989)
Carlos Ott, architect

COLONNE DE JUILLET
(base, 1833; column, 1840)
Jean-Antoine Alavoine, architect, base;
Joseph-Louis Duc, architect, column

5
OPÉRA BASTILLE (1989)
Carlos Ott, architect

For years the Place de la Bastille was an overlooked corner of Paris, a site more well known for the absence
of a specific building than for the presence of one. Haunted by history, the open public space was redolent
of memories of one of history's most memorable confluences of event and place: the storming of the
Bastille on July 14, 1789. The seizure of the Bastille marked a decisive moment in the incipient French
Revolution. Despised as an embodiment of monarchial absolutism and injustice, the building was destroyed
a year later. Today, where an angry mob once raged, orderly crowds now congregate to celebrate the arts in
the Opéra Bastille, the design of which was selected from among 787 schemes entered in an international
competition. At night, the building's heft gives way to luminosity, and the opera house becomes a beacon,
a glowing destination in the history-laden quarter of the Faubourg Saint-Antoine.

6
QUAI DE BÉTHUNE,
ÎLE SAINT-LOUIS,
(19th and 20th centuries)

PONT DE SULLY (1876)
Vaudrey & Brosselin, engineers

7

PONT ALEXANDRE III (1900)
Louis-Jean Résal and Amédée Alby, engineers; Henri Gauquié, sculptor of street lamp;
Léopold Morice, sculptor of *Le génie des eaux*

TOUR EIFFEL (1889)
Gustave Eiffel, engineer and builder

The most visually striking bridge built over the Seine during the nineteenth century is without a doubt the Pont Alexandre III, begun in 1895 and completed five years later as part of the facilities of the International Exposition of 1900. The bridge epitomizes the era of *la Belle Époque*. Though technologically innovative—it was one of the world's first bridges to be constructed of steel—the Pont Alexandre III disguises its functional essence as a conduit of traffic behind an unabashedly decorative façade. Lampposts incorporating angelic figures constitute monumentally scaled public sculptures, not mere lighting fixtures.
A brilliantly articulated set piece, the bridge turns ordinary comings and goings into charming scenes from an imaginary play or opera.

In contrast, Gustave Eiffel's tower, so iconic as to nearly defy being clearly seen and appreciated in formal terms, is indeed a work of art disguised as a work of engineering and commercialism. From its completion in 1889, the Tour Eiffel, has been immensely popular with the general public; it drew six million visitors in its first year. But Eiffel's success as an entrepreneur has to some extent overshadowed his artistic achievement; he created not only a bravura display of iron construction, but also a structure that both watches over the city and holds up the sky.

8
PONT ALEXANDRE III (1900)
Louis-Jean Résal and Amédée Alby, engineers;
Georges Gardet, sculptor of lion; H. Benozech, sculptor of urn

9
URN, PONT ALEXANDRE III (1900)
H. Benozech, sculptor

I O
PLACE DE LA CONCORDE (1755–1772)
Jacques-Ange Gabriel, architect;
Guillaume Ier Coustou, sculptor of the *Chevaux de Marly* (1746), replaced by cement copy, 1984;
Temporary structure in commemoration of the Liberation of Paris, Fiftieth Anniversary (1994),
with poster showing André Gander's photograph
FFI en position à la préfecture de Police de Paris—19–24 août 1944

Not only the city's virtual center in geographic terms, the Place de la Concorde is also the de facto
heart of Paris. Though it lacks the spatial definition and coherence of the Place des Vosges
(1606–1611), and is often choked with traffic, it remains the city's principal locus of movement and
one of the world's great urban outdoor spaces. First planned in 1755 on a then vacant site west of the
city, it was conceived by Jacques-Ange Gabriel as a "royal square" in honor of Louis XV.

The Place de la Concorde tells a story about Paris's past through a collection of monuments.
Guillaume Coustou's heroic equestrian statues were completed for the Abreuvoir de Marly in 1746,
moved to the western edge of the square, and replaced by cement copies in 1984. Reflecting the
hyperpractical and not especially poetic nature of our times, the deracinated sculptures are now
safely ensconced indoors at the Louvre, protected from the harmful man-made elements, but robbed
of their proud position at the terminus of the Champs-Élysées. Also denied its original context, the
thirteenth-century B.C. Obélisque de Louqsor stands as a testament not only to the power of ancient
Egypt, but also to that of nineteenth-century France: in 1831, Pasha Mehemet-Ali gave the
seventy-five-foot pink syenite monolith to Louis-Philippe. In the shadows of these monuments,
an immense poster announces an exhibition commemorating the fiftieth anniversary of the
liberation of Paris from Nazi occupation in 1944.

II
HÔTEL DE COISLIN, PLACE DE LA CONCORDE (1758)
Jacques-Ange Gabriel, architect

I 2
HÔTEL DE COISLIN, PLACE DE LA CONCORDE (1758)
Jacques-Ange Gabriel, architect

13
PLACE DE LA CONCORDE (1755–1772)
Jacques-Ange Gabriel, architect

OBÉLISQUE DE LOUQSOR (C. 1250 B.C.)
Jacques-Ignace Hittorff, reinstallation from
Egypt, 1831–1836

14
GRANDE ARCHE DE LA DÉFENSE (1989)
Johann Otto von Spreckelsen and Paul Andreu (Lauréat du concours), architects

15
GRANDE ARCHE DE LA DÉFENSE (1989)
Johann Otto von Spreckelsen and Paul Andreu (Lauréat du concours), architects

DÔME IMAX (1992)
Chaix Morel and Associates, architects

At once a humane habitat and a monument to power, Paris is also a city of abstractions, of pure geometries imagined and realized. The Grande Arche de la Défense constitutes a Modernist restatement of the triumphal arches at the Carrousel and the Étoile, and a contemporary equivalent to the Tour Eiffel, realizing the poetic potential of technology. Appearing to be a hollowed-out structure, nearly cubic in its dimensions, the arch incorporates two thirty-five-story office towers and is clad in Carrara marble, gray granite, and mirrored glass. Together with the nearby Dôme Imax, the arch establishes a Modernist monumentality as it resonates with the dreams of the eighteenth-century French architects Claude-Nicolas Ledoux and Étienne-Louis Boullée.

16

COUR D'HONNEUR, PALAIS-BOURBON (National Assembly), view to the north (1832)
Jules de Joly, architect; Walter de Maria, sculptor of monument to Bicentennial of the French
Revolution, 1789–1989 (1989–1990)

During the French Revolution, the Palais-Bourbon (1722), built by Louis XIV as a sumptuous home
for his daughter, was confiscated and renamed the Maison de la Révolution. Beginning in 1815 the
building, repeatedly expanded and altered, was occupied by the Chambre des Députés, the name of
which was changed in 1946 to the Assemblée Nationale. The building's architectural transformation
into a seat of government was completed in 1832. In 1989, to commemorate the bicentennial of the
Revolution, the artist Walter de Maria placed a twelve-ton gray granite sphere atop a Classical
limestone pedestal, which in turn surmounts a semicircular *table de lecture* that de Maria created from
an existing curved bench located in the building's entrance court. The sculpture's minimalism provides
a dramatic contrast to the building's complexly wrought grandeur, which mined the architectural past
to invoke imperial authority. In de Maria's work, the use of a rigorously structured formal vocabulary
suggests the timeless quality of humanistic values and ideals.

17
MUSÉE D'ART MODERNE DE LA VILLE DE PARIS (1937)
J.C. Dondel and Alfred Aubert, architects

18

MUSÉE D'ART MODERNE DE LA VILLE DE PARIS (1937)

J.C. Dondel and Alfred Aubert, architects; Antoine Bourdelle, sculptor of *Le génie de la France*;
Alfred Janniot, sculptor of bas relief *Les forces de la mer et de la terre*

Built for the International Exposition of 1937, but always intended to outlast the fair, the Musée d'Art Moderne
de la Ville de Paris offered a stripped-down Classical vocabulary that was at once reassuringly familiar in its
basic elements and, like a streamlined machine built for efficiency, forward looking in its minimalism.
Nearly devoid of architectural ornament, the building effectively serves as an armature for relief sculptures.

19

MUSÉE D'ORSAY (formerly Gare d'Orsay) (1900)

Victor Alexandre Laloux, architect

The Gare d'Orsay was completed in 1900 to provide visitors to the International Exposition fairgrounds with a grand entrance to a special, albeit temporary, world of invention and entertainment. But for much of the twentieth century, the railroad station far surpassed that specific *fin-de-siècle* goal, serving as an antechamber to the great stage that is Paris itself, hinting at the urban spectacle that will follow. Threatened with demolition following the cessation of railroad service in 1973, it was saved and its exterior meticulously restored. Today, the building, with its imposing Beaux-Arts façades, houses an incomparable collection of decorative and fine art.

20

RESTAURANT LEDOYEN, CHAMPS-ÉLYSÉES (1842)

Garden façade, *Les Cariatiades*; Jacques-Ignace Hittorff, architect

How appropriate that in a city where the pursuit of pleasure is treated with utmost seriousness, a
restaurant was designed by an architect whose scholarly interests in polychromy led to a widespread
reassessment of ancient Greek architecture. But Jacques-Ignace Hittorff was not archeological in his
approach to design, freely mixing Classical- and Renaissance-inspired elements to create a highly
eclectic whole, both rigorous and fanciful.

21
PALAIS
DE LA LÉGION
D'HONNEUR (1786)
Interior. Pierre Rousseau,
architect

22
JARDIN DE LA VILLA
SUISSE (1900)
Comte Alphonse Emmanuel
de Moncel de Perrin, sculptor
of *Alfred de Musset, Le rêve
du poète*

PALAIS DE LA
DÉCOUVERTE (1900)
Henri Deglane, architect

23
UNIVERSITÉ
DE PARIS, FACULTÉ
DES LETTRES ET DES
SCIENCES HUMAINES
(1900)
Henri Deglane, architect;
Georges Récipon, sculptor
of *Immortalité devançant
le temps*

24
JARDIN DES TUILERIES
(1664)
André Le Nôtre,
landscape architect
François Barois, sculptor of
Pomone (1696)

25
PONT MIRABEAU (1893)
Louis-Jean Résal and Amédée Alby, engineers
Jean Antoine Injalbert, sculptor of *L'Abondance*

Each bridge over the Seine is unique. Each is beautiful. Each provides us with a sense that crossing the river carries with it a greater significance: that safe passage is not a mundane feature of daily life, but a poetic fragment of a journey through time. The Pont Mirabeau's technological forms are more apparent than are those of some of Paris's other bridges. It also incorporates exuberant Beaux-Arts elements. The bridge's graceful structure, rendered in steel, carries forcefully modeled and sculpted ornament, including heraldic figures that joyfully celebrate arrivals and departures. The bridge does not seem merely to span the river; rather it appears to skip across the water. Simultaneously an efficient machine for moving traffic and a work of art of great visual interest and charm, the bridge's nascent Modernism wears a cloak of tradition. Yet it works as a whole, a cohesive and compelling architectural feature both on the river and within the city.

26

LA FLAMME DE LA LIBERTÉ, TUNNEL DE L'ALMA (1886/1989)

Copy of Frédéric Auguste Bartholdi's "Statue of Liberty"; Philippe Mathieu, architect of the 1989 monument, initiated by the *International Herald Tribune*; the Métalliers Champenois, foundry; Embellissements Gohard, guilder

In 1987, to celebrate its centennial the *International Herald Tribune* established a fund to produce an exact replica of the sculpted flame that adorns the Statue of Liberty to give as a gift to the city of Paris. Frédéric Auguste Bartholdi's immense sculpture, officially titled *Liberty Enlightening the World*, was completed on Bedloe's Island in the New York Harbor in 1886. One hundred and three years later, *La flamme de la liberté*, made of hammered brass covered in gold leaf, was installed on the Place de l'Alma. The replica was created from a wood-and-plaster mold used in the restoration of the Statue of Liberty. The flame is now more than a fragment of a colossus; it embodies a long process of exchange, material and intellectual, between two great nations.

27

PONT DE BIR-HAKEIM (originally Passerelle de Passy) (1900)
Louis Biette, engineer; Holger Wederkinch, sculptor of *La France renaissante* (1930)

AMBASSADE D'AUSTRALIE (1977)
Harry Seidler and Associates, architects

In 1930, Holger Wederkinch's figurative sculpture *La France renaissante* was completed and placed at one end of Louis Biette's Passerelle de Passy, later renamed the Pont de Bir-Hakeim. So dramatically caught in motion is the equestrian figure that it seems nearly poised to take flight, reflecting the irrepressible aspirations of a nation. France, having suffered the devastation of the "war to end all wars," dreamed of the future, and placed its hopes at the water's edge.

28

COUR PUGET, AILE RICHELIEU, MUSÉE DU LOUVRE (1993)

Martin Desjardins, sculptor of *Les captifs du piédestal de la statue de Louis XIV, Place des Victoires* (1685)

Within the confines of grand open spaces, elegantly articulated outdoor rooms, and the courtyards of great buildings, Paris ingeniously fulfills the potential of urban form to serve as a frame for art. Scattered throughout the city, figures of marble and bronze reflect the enduring power of the art object, not only as a product of the human imagination, but also as a means of defining a sense of place: the artwork as landmark. Individually distinctive, Paris's sculpted figures collectively imbue the city with an idealized human dimension, as they seemingly bear silent witness to the passage of time.

29
JARDIN DES TUILERIES
(1664)
André Le Nôtre, landscape
architect
Carlés Antonin, sculptor of
Retour de chasse (1888)

30
JARDIN DU CHAMP-DE-MARS (1908)
Jean-Camille Formigé, architect; Yvan Theimer, sculptor of *Monument des Droits de l'Homme et du Citoyen* (1989)

31
PAVILLON
MARSAN,
UNION
DES ARTS
DÉCORATIFS
(1882)
Hector Martin Lefuel,
architect

32
GRANDS MOULINS DE PARIS (19th century)

33
GRANDS MOULINS DE PARIS (19th century)

34
MINISTÈRE DES FINANCES
(1989)
Paul Chemetov and Borja
Huidobro, architects

**BIBLIOTHÈQUE
NATIONALE DE FRANCE
FRANÇOIS MITTERRAND**
(1997)
Dominique Perrault, architect

PONT DE BERCY (1864)
Féline-Romany, engineer

35
BIBLIOTHÈQUE NATIONALE DE FRANCE FRANÇOIS MITTERRAND (1997)
Dominique Perrault, architect; Chaix Morel and Associates, architects of temporary "tepee"

The Bibliothèque Nationale de France François Mitterrand, which can house up to 12 million books, is the
largest of the *Grands Projets*. Clad in glass, the building evokes the visions of early twentieth-century
Modernist architects. Four L-shaped towers of twenty-five stories each rise from their riverside site to
become a dominant feature of the skyline. The towers, which suggest open books,
house reading rooms defined by panels of exotic wood.

36
MINISTÈRE DES FINANCES (1989)
Paul Chemetov and Borja Huidobro, architects

In 1989, the Ministère des Finances, which had occupied the Richelieu Wing of the Louvre, moved to an imposing new megastructural building. Containing close to 300,000 square feet of office space, the massive building makes a strong statement about governmental power. Europe's first large-scale, precabled building, it also celebrates a technological future. But it is the building's relationship to the Seine that is perhaps most memorable. The river is no longer an obstacle to be crossed, as it was in 1864 when the Pont de Bercy was completed. Today the riverside highway is a tear in the urban fabric that needs to be negotiated and the river has become a visual reward to be savored periodically throughout a hectic workday.

37
PALAIS OMNISPORTS DE PARIS-BERCY (1983)
Michel Andrault and Pierre Parat, architects

Like I.M. Pei's masterful addition to the Louvre, the Palais Omnisports de Paris-Bercy utilizes a pyramidal form, as well as subterranean construction, to create a monumental structure that is both visually dramatic and functionally efficient. Designed to house a wide range of events, from tennis matches to concerts, the stadium can seat 17,000 spectators in a truncated hexagonal pyramid surmounted by a metal-and-glass space frame carried on four nearly seventeen-foot-wide concrete columns. A large portion of the building's sloping exterior walls, angled at forty-five degrees, is covered with grass, transforming the behemoth into a natural complement to the river and the nearby Parc de Bercy.

38
ÉCOLE NATIONALE SUPÉRIEURE DES BEAUX-ARTS
(1816–1832; 1858–1862)
F. Debret and Jacques-Felix Duban, architects

The École Nationale Supérieure des Beaux-Arts—whose faculty and alumni exerted such a tremendous impact on the history of architecture internationally that an entire architectural vocabulary bears its name—is itself a kind of museum of French architecture. Here, architecture served didactic as well as aesthetic goals, and the past served as a springboard for a highly inventive, invigorated, and influential Classicism.

39
BIBLIOTHÈQUE
DE L'ARSENAL
(1594)
Philibert Delorme,
architect

40

PALAIS DE CHAILLOT (1937)

Jacques Carlu, Leon Azéma, and Louis-Hippolyte Boileau, architects;

Pierre-Marie Poisson, sculptor of *Jeunesse*

The Palais de Chaillot, built for the International Exposition of 1937, crowns a hilltop adjacent
to the Seine with two curved wings that conform to the footprint of a former building on
the site, the Palais du Trocadéro, built for the International Exposition of 1878. Between the two
wings, which now house museums, a terraced plaza acts as an *agora* that is as significant in
its civic function as the building complex itself. Integrating architecture and art,
building and landscape, and Classicism and Modernism, the complex serves as a compelling,
accessible setting for shared urban experience.

41
FAÇADE OCCIDENTALE, PALAIS DE JUSTICE (1868)
Joseph-Louis Duc, architect

Few sites in Paris boast longer recorded histories and few buildings speak more forcefully of
French political traditions than the Palais de Justice. Occupying a large site on the Île de la Cité
that during the Roman Empire contained a Governor's Palace, this vast complex of buildings
incorporates medieval landmarks including Sainte-Chapelle (1242–1248) and the Conciergerie
(begun in the fourteenth century). The Façade Occidentale of the Palais de Justice, built under
the reign of Napoleon III, boldly replaced the third side of the intimately scaled Place Dauphine,
and adopted a succinctly articulated Neoclassical vocabulary. Restrained in its design,
the building established a sense of imperial stability—and, its builders hoped, permanence.
Here was a public building that powerfully expressed government authority. The Façade
Occidentale was clear—nearly reductivist—in its geometries. Despite the coolly Classical whole
that looked back to the ancient temples at Stratonice and Denderah, however, the façade mixed
traditional elements with romantic, figurative sculptures and details. A rhythmically insistent row
of engaged columns was punctuated by large expanses of glass, while the overall composition
was enlivened by monumental staircases.

42

COUR D'HONNEUR, PALAIS-BOURBON (National Assembly), view to the south (1832)
Barreau de Chefdeville, architect

43
**GRANDE GALERIE DE
L'ÉVOLUTION, MUSÉUM
NATIONAL
D'HISTOIRE NATURELLE**
(1889)
Jules André, architect of the exterior;
Transformation of the interior, the
Grande Galerie de l'Évolution, Paul
Chemetov and Borja Huidobro,
architects (1994); Claude Guillaume,
sculptor of *Histoire Naturelle*, *Guy
Crescent Fagon* and *Guy de la Brosse*

44
PONT-NEUF (1578–1607)
Androuet du Cerceau l'aîné and Guillaume Marchant, architects

LA SAMARITAINE (1928)
Henri Sauvage and Frantz Jourdan, architects

Despite its name, the Pont-Neuf is the oldest existent bridge in Paris. Begun by Henri III in 1578, the bridge is in fact two spans interrupted by the triangular western end of the Île de la Cité. Construction was halted by the Wars of Religion, and when it was resumed by Henri IV, whose extensive building initiatives dramatically modernized Paris, the design was radically changed. Like all of Paris's bridges at the time, the Pont-Neuf was originally flanked by dense rows of houses. Under the direction of Henri IV, the Pont-Neuf became the first bridge in Paris where houses were replaced by walkways. A series of semicircular projections soon served as gathering places for entertainers, peddlers, even dentists, who set up booths or worked in the open air. More than a bridge, the Pont-Neuf functioned as a city square. In time, the focus of attention shifted from the bridge to the river itself, and the Pont-Neuf became less of a stage and more of a parquet within a larger urban theater, serving as an ideal place from which to watch the river and the city beyond. Opening itself to unobstructed views, the Pont-Neuf set a precedent for the city's subsequent bridges and established a key feature of the city's form and character.

45
PONT DU CARROUSEL
(1935–1939)
Malet & Lang, engineers;
Raymond Subes, artisan of *Obélisques*
télescopiques (light column) (1959);
Louis Petitot, sculptor of *La Seine*
and *La Ville de Paris* (1846)

PAVILLON DE FLORE,
MUSÉE DU LOUVRE (1861)
Hector Martin Lefuel, architect

46
RÉSIDENCE
PASSY-KENNEDY,
LE TRIPODE (1990)
André Remondet,
architect

TOUR EIFFEL (1889)
Gustave Eiffel, engineer

47
MAISON DE RADIO-FRANCE (1963)
Henri Bernard, architect

HORLOGE DE LA MAISON DE RADIO-FRANCE (1988)
Enterprise Bideau, designer

The Maison de Radio-France is an efficient tool for radio and television
broadcasting; nearly 2,500 people work within its circular structure, 175 meters
in diameter. Clad in aluminum panels, the building evokes its era's high-tech
modes of transportation—ocean liners and jets—in an appropriate metaphor for
the transmission of culture and ideas at the dawn of the Information Age.
Sleek and built for efficiency, the building also hearkens back to an earlier time;
a tower nearly 200 feet high, housing the network's archives, serves as a
modern-day equivalent to a church's campanile.

48
NOTRE-DAME DE PARIS
(1162–1344, 1841–1879)
Various architects; Jean Ravy,
architect of *chevet* (1318–1344);
Eugène Emmanuel Viollet-le-Duc,
architect of *flèche* (1844–1879)

PONT DE L'ARCHEVÊCHÉ
(1828)
Plouard, engineer

Notre-Dame de Paris, begun in 1162,
has served as a visual anchor for
the city throughout centuries of
perpetual and often tumultuous
urban growth and change.
A pioneering and preeminent
exemplar of Gothic architecture,
the cathedral exerts a powerful
presence in a city replete with
monuments. Successive building
campaigns and radical stylistic and
technological innovations, including
the flying buttress, rendered the
building a masterpiece.
Eugène Emmanuel Viollet-le-Duc's
controversial restoration,
completed in 1879, added the
visually dominant *flèche*.

49
QUAI D'ORLÉANS, ÎLE SAINT-LOUIS (19th and 20th centuries)

50
ÉGLISE DU DÔME
(DÔME DES INVALIDES)
(1679–1708)
Jules Hardouin-Mansart, architect

51
SERRE,
PARC ANDRÉ-CITROËN
(1992)
Patrick Berger, architect;
Gilles Clément, landscape
architect

52
SERRE, PARC ANDRÉ-CITROËN (1992)
Patrick Berger, architect; Gilles Clément, landscape architect

A part of the Parc André-Citroën, located on the former site of an automobile factory, a greenhouse—one of a pair—provides a focal point terminating the vista across the geometrically arranged park. Here the forms of industrial architecture are echoed, but adapted to a diametrically opposed purpose: not the manufacture of machines but the cultivation of plants. Within the structures' seemingly fragile glass walls, carried on slender but visually dominant wooden columns, nature reigns in an apt encapsulation of the park itself. Thirty-two acres large, and as long as the Champ-de-Mars, the park is a welcome intrusion into the surrounding urban fabric of apartment developments, office complexes, multi-lane roadways, and railroad tracks.

53
ATRIUM DU THÉÂTRE DES CHAMPS-ÉLYSÉES (1923)
Henry Van de Velde and Auguste Perret, architects; Antoine Bourdelle, sculptor of *Pénéloppe* (1923)

54
CANAL PLUS (1991)
Richard Meier and Partners, architects

55
PARC DE BERCY
(1995)
Bernard Huet and
Marylène Ferrand,
architects;
Ian le Caisne and
Philippe Raguin,
landscape architects

56
PARC DE BERCY (1995)
Bernard Huet and Marylène Ferrand, architects; Ian le Caisne and Philippe Raguin, landscape architects

57
PARC DE BERCY (1995)
Bernard Huet and Marylène Ferrand, architects; Ian le Caisne and Philippe Raguin, landscape architects

Replacing the Entrepôt des Vins, a sprawling district of nineteenth-century warehouses and storage cellars
serving the wine industry, the Parc de Bercy has come to life as a tranquil oasis that is at once distinctly modern
and steeped in memories—both of the former industrial precinct it replaced and of the traditions of French
landscape design. The park retains physical traces of the old district, including cobblestone-paved streets,
mature trees, and one of the wine cellars, which has now been restored. The park, densely layered in both
visual and historical terms, is divided into distinct areas, including an open lawn that contrasts with carefully
composed flower gardens. Parterres and promenades add a crisp, geometrical dimension evocative of the
seventeenth-century work of André Le Nôtre.

58

HIPPODROME DE LONGCHAMP (1967)

Jacques Regnault, architect

59
SERRE TROPICALE, JARDIN DES PLANTES,
MUSÉUM NATIONAL D'HISTOIRE NATURELLE (1937)
René Berger, architect

The Serre Tropicale in the Jardin des Plantes, completed in 1937, marries the forms and compositional
principles of Classicism to the materials and aesthetics of the Machine Age. The resulting essay in Modern
Classicism, rendered in glass and steel, is powerful in its purity. The uninterrupted sweep of its enveloping
form suggests the protective environment of a grotto, yet its transparent walls allow natural light to nurture
the plants inside, as nature and artifice conduct a complex conversation.

60
JARDIN
DES SERRES
D'AUTEUIL,
BOIS DE
BOULOGNE
(1895–1897)
Jean-Camille Formigé,
architect; Schwarz &
Meurer, engineers

61
JARDIN DES SERRES D'AUTEUIL, BOIS DE BOULOGNE (1895–1897)
Jean-Camille Formigé, architect; Schwarz & Meurer, engineers

In the Jardin des Serres d'Auteuil in the Bois de Boulogne, nature provides a backdrop for
quiet contemplation at the edge of the inner city. But nature is here not merely conserved.
The gardens serve an important municipal function, containing the nurseries that supply
the greenery for parks and gardens throughout Paris. Additionally, the gardens serve
a didactic purpose, providing public educational programs. Architecture sets the stage
for cultivation in an extensive series of gardens and greenhouses, including a
fifty-two-foot high, domed palm house.

62
PAVILLON DE L'HORLOGE, BOIS DE BOULOGNE (1777)
François-Joseph Bélanger, architect

A Pavillon de l'Horloge—one of a pair adjacent to the Château de Bagatelle—is the perfect architectural complement to a great house-and-garden complex. The small but carefully proportioned building is finely articulated and detailed so as to appear at once stately and charming. Incorporating a clock and surmounted by a compass, the building serves multiple functional purposes, but never loses sight of its role as a garden pavilion existing calmly beneath towering chestnut trees.

63
AMERICAN CENTER (1994)
Frank O. Gehry and Associates, architects

64
PONT ALEXANDRE III (1900)
Louis-Jean Résal and
Amédée Alby, engineers

Like the heavenly city described in the *Book of Revelation*, Paris is a place that a river runs through. The dialogue between the Seine and the surrounding city has always been a principal source of Paris's allure. So integral to the city is the Seine, that one can imagine it not merely as a backdrop for the unfolding human drama, but as a participant in it: the Seine is an inanimate observer that has seen all that has taken place on its banks and it will see all that the future will bring.

For more than two millennia, the complex, collective, and constantly changing work of art that is the city of Paris—its buildings, its bridges, its river, its light—has cast its spell.

KEY TO THE MAP BY PLATE NUMBER

1
COUR NAPOLÉON,
MUSÉE DU LOUVRE
PYRAMIDE DU LOUVRE

2
PYRAMIDE DU LOUVRE

3
PYRAMIDE DU LOUVRE
COUR NAPOLÉON,
MUSÉE DU LOUVRE

4
OPÉRA BASTILLE
COLONNE DE JUILLET

5
OPÉRA BASTILLE

6
QUAI DE BÉTHUNE,
ÎLE SAINT-LOUIS
PONT DE SULLY

7
PONT ALEXANDRE III
TOUR EIFFEL

8
PONT ALEXANDRE III

9
URN, PONT ALEXANDRE III

10
PLACE DE LA CONCORDE

11
HÔTEL DE COISLIN,
PLACE DE LA CONCORDE

12
HÔTEL DE COISLIN,
PLACE DE LA CONCORDE

13
PLACE DE LA CONCORDE
OBÉLISQUE DE LOUQSOR

14
GRANDE ARCHE DE LA DÉFENSE

15
GRANDE ARCHE DE LA DÉFENSE
DÔME IMAX

16
COUR D'HONNEUR,
PALAIS-BOURBON

17
MUSÉE D'ART MODERNE
DE LA VILLE DE PARIS

18
MUSÉE D'ART MODERNE
DE LA VILLE DE PARIS

19
MUSÉE D'ORSAY

20
RESTAURANT LEDOYEN,
CHAMPS-ÉLYSÉES

21
PALAIS DE LA LÉGION D'HONNEUR

22
JARDIN DE LA VILLA SUISSE
PALAIS DE LA DÉCOUVERTE

23
UNIVERSITÉ DE PARIS, FACULTÉ
DES LETTRES ET DES SCIENCES
HUMAINES

24
JARDIN DES TUILERIES

25
PONT MIRABEAU

26
LA FLAMME DE LA LIBERTÉ,
TUNNEL DE L'ALMA

27
PONT DE BIR-HAKEIM
AMBASSADE D'AUSTRALIE

28
COUR PUGET, AILE RICHELIEU,
MUSÉE DU LOUVRE

29
JARDIN DES TUILERIES

30
JARDIN DU CHAMP-DE-MARS

31
PAVILLON MARSAN,
UNION DES ARTS DÉCORATIFS

32
GRANDS MOULINS DE PARIS

33
GRANDS MOULINS DE PARIS

34
MINISTÈRE DES FINANCES
BIBLIOTHÈQUE NATIONALE DE
FRANCE FRANÇOIS MITTERRAND
PONT DE BERCY

35
BIBLIOTHÈQUE NATIONALE DE
FRANCE FRANÇOIS MITTERRAND

36
MINISTÈRE DES FINANCES

37
PALAIS OMNISPORTS DE
PARIS-BERCY

38
ÉCOLE NATIONALE SUPÉRIEURE
DES BEAUX-ARTS

39
BIBLIOTHÈQUE DE L'ARSENAL

40
PALAIS DE CHAILLOT

41
FAÇADE OCCIDENTALE,
PALAIS DE JUSTICE

42
COUR D'HONNEUR,
PALAIS-BOURBON

43
GRANDE GALERIE DE
L'ÉVOLUTION, MUSÉUM NATIONAL
D'HISTOIRE NATURELLE

44
PONT-NEUF
LA SAMARITAINE

45
PONT DU CARROUSEL
PAVILLON DE FLORE,
MUSÉE DU LOUVRE

46
RÉSIDENCE PASSY-KENNEDY,
LE TRIPODE
TOUR EIFFEL

47
MAISON DE RADIO-FRANCE
HORLOGE DE LA MAISON DE
RADIO-FRANCE

48
NOTRE-DAME DE PARIS
PONT DE L'ARCHEVÊCHÉ

49
QUAI D'ORLÉANS, ÎLE SAINT-LOUIS

50
ÉGLISE DU DÔME
(DÔME DES INVALIDES)

51
SERRE, PARC ANDRÉ-CITROËN

52
SERRE, PARC ANDRÉ-CITROËN

53
ATRIUM DU THÉÂTRE
DES CHAMPS-ÉLYSÉES

54
CANAL PLUS

55
PARC DE BERCY

56
PARC DE BERCY

57
PARC DE BERCY

58
HIPPODROME DE LONGCHAMP

59
SERRE TROPICALE,
JARDIN DES PLANTES,
MUSÉUM NATIONAL D'HISTOIRE
NATURELLE

60
JARDIN DES SERRES D'AUTEUIL,
BOIS DE BOULOGNE

61
JARDIN DES SERRES D'AUTEUIL,
BOIS DE BOULOGNE

62
PAVILLON DE L'HORLOGE,
BOIS DE BOULOGNE

63
AMERICAN CENTER

64
PONT ALEXANDRE III

CHANGING PARIS

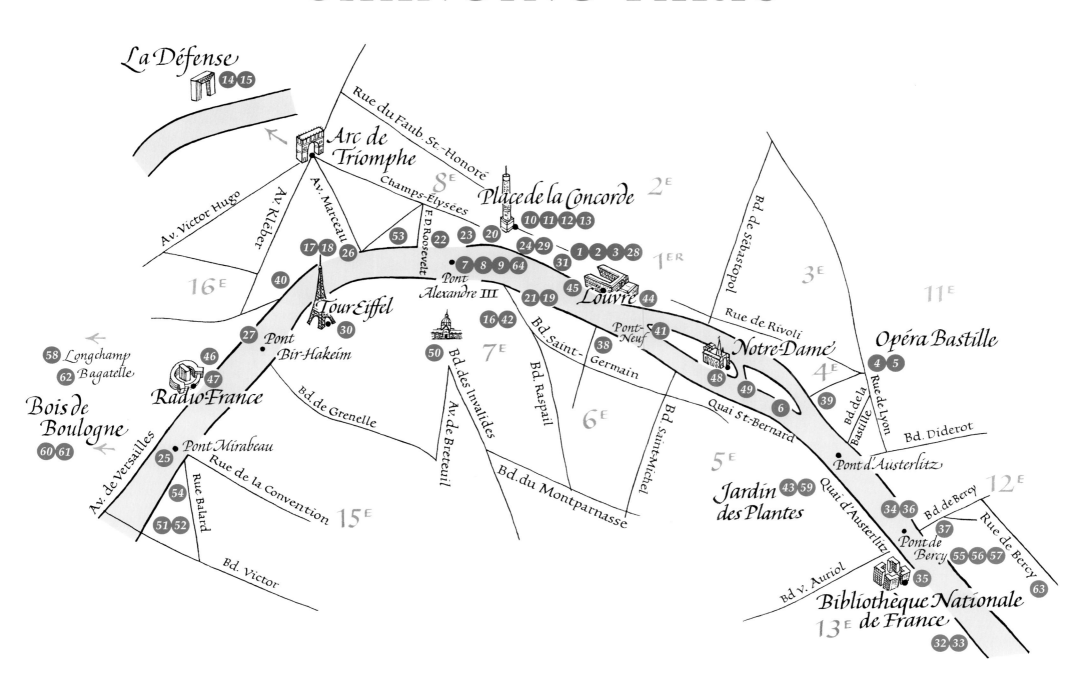

ALPHABETIZED LIST OF SITES

AMBASSADE D'AUSTRALIE
Métro *Bir-Hakeim*

AMERICAN CENTER
Métro *Bercy*

ATRIUM DU THÉÂTRE DES
CHAMPS-ÉLYSÉES
Métro *Alma-Marceau*

BIBLIOTHÈQUE
DE L'ARSENAL
Métro *Sully-Morland*

BIBLIOTHÈQUE NATIONALE
DE FRANCE
FRANÇOIS MITTERRAND
Métro *Bibliothèque François
Mitterrand*

CANAL PLUS
Métro *Balard*

COLONNE DE JUILLET
Métro *Bastille*

COUR D'HONNEUR,
PALAIS-BOURBON
Métro *Assemblée-Nationale*

COUR NAPOLÉON,
MUSÉE DU LOUVRE
Métro *Palais Royal Musée du
Louvre*

COUR PUGET,
AILE RICHELIEU,
MUSÉE DU LOUVRE
Métro *Palais Royal Musée du
Louvre*

DÔME IMAX
Métro *Grande Arche de la
Défense*

ÉCOLE NATIONALE
SUPÉRIEURE DES
BEAUX-ARTS
Métro *Saint-Germain-
des-Prés*

ÉGLISE DU DÔME
(DÔME DES INVALIDES)
Métro *Varenne*

FAÇADE OCCIDENTALE,
PALAIS DE JUSTICE
Métro *Cité*

LA FLAMME DE LA LIBERTÉ,
TUNNEL DE L'ALMA
Métro *Alma-Marceau*

GRANDE ARCHE DE LA
DÉFENSE
Métro *Grande Arche de la
Défense*

GRANDE GALERIE DE
L'ÉVOLUTION, MUSÉUM
NATIONAL
D'HISTOIRE NATURELLE
Métro *Place Monge*

GRANDS MOULINS DE PARIS
Métro *Bibliothèque François
Mitterrand*

HIPPODROME DE
LONGCHAMP
Métro *La Muette*

HORLOGE DE LA MAISON
DE RADIO-FRANCE
Métro *Passy*

HÔTEL DE COISLIN, PLACE
DE LA CONCORDE
Métro *Concorde*

JARDIN DE LA VILLA
SUISSE
Métro *Franklin D. Roosevelt*

JARDIN DES SERRES
D'AUTEUIL,
BOIS DE BOULOGNE
Métro *Porte d'Auteuil*

JARDIN DES TUILERIES
Métro *Tuileries*

JARDIN DU CHAMP-DE-
MARS
Métro *Bir-Hakeim*

MAISON DE RADIO-FRANCE
Métro *Passy*

MINISTÈRE DES FINANCES
Métro *Bercy*

MUSÉE D'ART MODERNE DE
LA VILLE DE PARIS
Métro *Alma-Marceau*

MUSÉE D'ORSAY
Métro *Solférino*

NOTRE-DAME DE PARIS
Métro *Cité*

OBÉLISQUE DE LOUQSOR
Métro *Concorde*

OPÉRA BASTILLE
Métro *Bastille*

PALAIS DE CHAILLOT
Métro *Trocadéro*

PALAIS DE LA DÉCOUVERTE
Métro *Franklin D. Roosevelt*

PALAIS DE LA LÉGION
D'HONNEUR
Métro *Solférino*

PALAIS OMNISPORTS DE
PARIS-BERCY
Métro *Bercy*

PARC DE BERCY
Métro *Bercy*

PAVILLON DE FLORE,
MUSÉE DU LOUVRE
Métro *Palais Royal Musée
du Louvre*

PAVILLON DE L'HORLOGE,
BOIS DE BOULOGNE
Métro *Porte d'Auteuil*

PAVILLON MARSAN, UNION
DES ARTS DÉCORATIFS
Métro *Palais Royal Musée du
Louvre*

PLACE DE LA CONCORDE
Métro *Concorde*

PONT ALEXANDRE III
Métro *Invalides*

PONT DE BERCY
Métro *Bercy*

PONT DE BIR-HAKEIM
Métro *Bir-Hakeim*

PONT DE L'ARCHEVÊCHÉ
Métro *Cité*

PONT DE SULLY
Métro *Sully-Morland*

PONT DU CARROUSEL
Métro *Palais Royal Musée du
Louvre*

PONT MIRABEAU
Métro *Mirabeau*

PONT-NEUF
Métro *Pont-Neuf*

PYRAMIDE DU LOUVRE
Métro *Palais Royal Musée du
Louvre*

QUAI DE BÉTHUNE,
ÎLE SAINT-LOUIS
Métro *Cité*

QUAI D'ORLÉANS,
ÎLE SAINT-LOUIS
Métro *Cité*

RÉSIDENCE PASSY-
KENNEDY, LE TRIPODE
Métro *Passy*

RESTAURANT LEDOYEN,
CHAMPS-ÉLYSÉES
Métro *Champs-Élysées
Clemenceau*

LA SAMARITAINE
Métro *Pont-Neuf*

SERRE,
PARC ANDRÉ-CITROËN
Métro *Balard*

SERRE TROPICALE,
JARDIN DES PLANTES,
MUSÉUM NATIONAL
D'HISTOIRE NATURELLE
Métro *Place Monge*

TOUR EIFFEL
Métro *Bir-Hakeim*

UNIVERSITÉ DE PARIS,
FACULTÉ DES LETTRES ET
DES SCIENCES HUMAINES
Métro *Champs-Élysées
Clemenceau*

URN, PONT ALEXANDRE III
Métro *Champs-Élysées
Clemenceau*

Plate 10: Photograph in the colonnade: *FFI en position à la préfecture de Police de Paris—19–24 août 1944;* André Gander, photographer, Musée de la Libération de Paris—50ème anniversaire (1994), made available by the agency Sagacité

Plates 11 and 12: Hôtel de Coislin, Concorde International

Plates 16 and 42: Palais-Bourbon: authorization given by MM. les Questeurs

Plates 22, 24, 29, 30, 51, 52, 55, 56, 57, 60, 61, and 62: Maîtrise d'ouvage: Direction des Parcs, Jardins et Espaces verts de la Ville de Paris

Plate 47: Maison de Radio-France (1963): architect: Henri Bernard © Adagp, Paris 1997

Plate 58: L'Hippodrome de Longchamp: Domaine de la Ville de Paris

CHANGING PARIS: A TOUR ALONG THE SEINE

was designed and typeset in Fournier by Katy Homans.

The duotone separations were made by Robert J. Hennessey.

The map was drawn by Jerry Kelly.

The books were printed and bound by Martino Mardersteig
at Stamperia Valdonega, Verona, Italy.

A limited edition of this book, of 100 copies,
each in a clamshell box
with a signed and numbered photograph printed in platinum/palladium metals,
is available through Arena Editions.